A BOY WITH MANY DREAMS

Dreams are small and Dreams are big.Once there was a boy name Little Jay.Little Jay had very big dreams.He wondered what his life would be like.He dreamed of being a wrestler,a football player,and a basketball player too.Poor little Jay was very confussed,so he went to the kitchen to find his mother.He asked his mother for some advice.`Mom,what am I to do with my life?"

Mom turned to Little Jay and said, `You can be anything you want be,and whatever you decide,I will be proud of you.'

`Thanks,mom,' Little Jay said.But he was still confussed.So Little Jay went to ask his father for advice.

Little Jay went into his father's study and found his father sitting at his desk.Litttle Jay said,`Dad,I need your advice.What am I to do with my life?'Little Jay's father raised his head,looked at Little Jay, and said,`Well,son,you know that I would like you to be a basketball player just like me,but whatever you choose,I will be proud of you.' `Thanks,Dad,'Little Jay said.But he was still confussed.

`Well,well,well,'Little Jay said to himself,`What am I to do with my life?'Little Jay headed off to his room.It was time for bed.`School is tomorrow.I will ask my friends and teachers what am I to do with my life,'he thought.Then he crawled into bed and was fast asleeep.

Little Jay dreamed that he was a wrestler.He dreamed that he was wrestling against his favorite wrestler.Suddenly,Little Jay stopped the match,looked at his favorite wrestler,and asked,`What am I to do with my life?'

The wrestler looked down at little jay and said,`It's cool that you want to be a wrestler just like me,but it's up to you to decide.

`Thanks,'said little jay.But he was still confused.He shook his head and turned to walk away.When he turned to say goodbye,his favorite wrestler was nowhere to be found.When Little Jay awoke from his dream the next morning,he was still confused.

Little Jay went off to school to ask his friends and teachers what he should do with his life.as he walked into the classroom,he spotted his best friend Dave.Little jay asked Dave, `Hey,Dave what am I to do with my life? Should I be a wrestler,a football player,or a basketball player?'

Dave answered, `Do whatever you like! You love football,basketball and wrestling,so whatever you choose will be alright.'

Little Jay said to Dave, `You know that I love basketball more.'

Dave said,I know.But you have to choose what to do. It's up to you to decide.

`Thanks,Dave,'said Little Jay. `You're my best friend.

But Little Jay was still confused.He could not decide what he wanted to do with his life.

The teacher walked in the classroom and smiled.she said,`Good morning, class!'

`Good morning,Mrs.Lumpkin!'shouted the children

`How is everyone today?'asked Mrs.Lumpkin

`We're fine!'everyone shouted

Mrs.Lumpkin asked,`Who remembers what I told you after class yesterday?'

All the children raised their hands.

`What did I say?'asked Mrs.Lumpkin

The whole class shouted together,`We can be anything we want to be,if we just believe in our dreams.'

Little Jay raised his hand.

`Yes,Little Jay?'Mrs. Lumpkin said.

`Mrs.Lumpkin,what am I to do with my life?'Little Jay asked.

Mrs.Lumpkin said to Little Jay,`Just remember my words.You can be anything you want to be,as long as you believe in your dreams.It's up to you to decide.'

`Thanks,Mrs. Lumpkin,'Little Jay said,`I think I have decided what I want to be.'

On his way home from school,Little Jay was filled with joy because he finally knew what he wanted to do with his life.When Little Jay walked into the house,he found his mom and dad.He looked at his parent and smiled.

`Mom and Dad,'he said, `I know I'm only nine and I have alots of time to decide,but I already know what I want to do with my life.I want to make you proud of me.So,after I finish high school,I will college and play football and basketball.One day I will be a football star.I will play for the New Orleans Saints with Drew Brees!

`I'm going to be a basketball star, too! I'm going to wear white and green.I'm going to play for the Boston Celtics!'

Little Jay smailed as he thought about what he would do with his life .

`Mom and dad,'one day you will see your lilttle boy living his dreams.'

After talking with his parent Lil Jay went to his

Room,sat on his bed and said

"man,what a day now I know what I want to

Be" I am happy

A famous basketball player with the team I so

Truly love the Boston Celtics, yes, a dream that

I will make come true.As soon as I finished high

school and I go to college.

While Lil Jay was in deep thought looking at

His Boston Celtics poster of Ray Allen and the

Whole team he didn't see Ray coming to life.

"Hey,lil man, how are you", say Ray

Lil Jay look up and see Ray,turn and said,

"hey,man your not real.

"Yes! I am",Ray said.

I was sent here to tell you

That you made a good choice.

"I did",said Lil Jay

Yeah!,man said Ray

It's cool you wanna be a basketball player

I been watching over you since you was little.

"Well how you know I was gonna choose

Basketball",said Lil Jay

Cause we have been watching over you

Ever since you first wanted to play basketball.

"But, I'm to short, do you think

I'll be able to play at all", said Lil Jay

"Well I'm pretty sure you will

Cause there someone in the NBA

Now who is very short and plays very well",said Ray

"That's is soooo cool and he is short

like me",said Lil Jay

"It's very cool,but you got to

remember that Education is good also"said Ray

"I know", said Lil Jay

And I promise to do my

best at keeping my grades up in high school and

college.

"That the right thing I want to

hear you say",said Ray

"And remember put God first in everything
You do,cause he will help you to keep your
dream real",said Ray.

"And I will",said Lil Jay

God is always first in may life that

How my dream will become my reality

Thank you so much,Mr. Ray Allen and your

whole team for watching and beliving in me.

"And